1

Published by Ambient Publishing.

ILLUSTRATIONS BY TOM SEARS *(www.tom-sears.com)*

"All of us have moments in our childhood where we come alive for the first time; and we go back to those moments and think, 'This is when I became myself.'"

Rita Dove

CONTENTS PAGE

HOW TO USE THIS BOOK AS A PARENT

Parents often fall into one of two camps, each as extreme as the other. In the first camp are those parents that underestimate the changes their child is about to encounter through the transition to a new school. These parents let the child 'do as they do' and play no part in the important journey their child is undertaking. In the second camp are those parents who panic in the face of this prospect of change. They think the best way to 'guide' their child successfully through school is to do the impossible: to hold their hand, all of the time.

This book shows you how to be the parent that takes the middle path between these two extremes. The philosophy underpinning this book is a simple one- childhood is intrinsically valuable. Your child will get only one childhood and, as parents, you simply must not allow your own fears and desires to overwhelm what would otherwise be a healthy, happy one. In short, the person you bought this book for should have a childhood *at least* as happy as it is 'successful'. The book itself is split into two sections; one for the child who must undergo the new journey through school, and one for the parent who must support them. It would be a mistake to think that parents are not active participants in this journey. As we shall see throughout this book, success at secondary school is often the result of a shared effort between child and parent. There are many things your child will need before he or she can even think about what we consider to be 'success' in this book- excelling in academic work, making friends, feeling valued- and some of those things will require your help, whether it be providing a good working environment back home, ensuring a good diet, or being the 'somebody' they can talk to when things go wrong. Be aware that your child craves the guided stewardship needed to grow into a young man or woman of the world, and that this book equips *you* with the necessary skills to play that role. Much of what you will find within the covers of this book is relevant to any child growing up, whether they have already undertaken the step up to secondary school, or are yet to do so.

Read the parental section first, before giving the book over to your child to read the student section. You are encouraged to make notes in the margins of the book, underlining key words or phrases that are most relevant for you. Encourage your child to do the same. We also strongly recommend that you take the time to read the student section - it is important that you appreciate the trials and tribulations your child will have to go through, and that you understand the help this book can offer them.

The book draws upon many years of experience from its authors, in their own roles as teacher, parent, student and child. Maria Adams has over 30 years experience teaching in secondary schools and a master's degree in Education with a specialism concerning children with learning difficulties. She also has a graduate diploma in Counseling. Martin Adams is a graduate of Harvard University as well as universities in both England and Australia. In addition to teaching in the UK, he has taught younger children in an orphanage in Cochabamba, Bolivia, and he is a Board Member at C.A.S.A- a non-profit network dedicated to representing the best interests of children who have been removed from their homes due to abuse or neglect. Together, they have taught children from ages 7 to 15, and run numerous innovative courses on study skills, child psychology and preparing children for their move to secondary school. More importantly, they have, together, undertaken the journey from primary to secondary school in the role of parent and child. Therefore, in truth, this book is a reflection of personal experience and discovered common sense more than any other academic discipline or insight. Its contents reflect mistakes made, as much as successes achieved.

INTRODUCTION

Let's cut right to it: the transition your child will undergo when moving from primary to secondary school can be as daunting and stressful for you as it can for them. However, it is crucial you do not let your anxiety affect your child's journey. As a parent you can be a very valuable source of advice, and even inspiration, for your child. By the time your child has finished reading their own section of this book they will be better prepared for secondary education and more receptive to any additional support you can offer them. So, read the parental section, digest its contents (however hard they seem to swallow) and look forward to playing a meaningful role at such a key time in your child's life.

A key point to remember is that although your child may not actively encourage you to be involved in their school life, it is still important that they are aware you are interested and are willing to support them. It may have been a long time since you yourself were at secondary school and so we aim to inform you on how things have progressed. But, you don't have to be a computer genius or even remember anything you learnt at school to be able to help your child through this transition and then on throughout their school years. You just need to *want to* be there for your child at this important stage in their life.

Every child will react differently to the changes in their lives; some will be excited, others scared. You know your child better than anyone, so don't underestimate your insight into their behaviour or the importance of your support. Luckily you will have support too, from the school, teachers, and parents of your child's friends, and of course this book.

Your child may seem stressed or unhappy in the build up to secondary school and the new workload once they arrive may get them down.

Things to look out for:

- Has your child become very quiet and withdrawn?
- Are they more angry or emotional than normal?
- Are they having trouble sleeping?
- Have they lost their appetite?

TOP TIPS:

- Take the time to sit down with them every day about how they are feeling and how school is going. It may take more than just one talk to get things out in the open, but persevere!
- Make sure they aren't staying up too late even if it's for school-work. 8-10hrs sleep is very important and they will need all their energy for the longer school day.
- For extra advice there are many organisations you can talk to such as www.youngminds.co.uk which gives you valuable tips to de-stress your child.

1. FINDING THE RIGHT SCHOOL FOR YOUR CHILD

Which school will your child attend? If you have not yet made the decision about your child's school then this section will help you do just that. If you have made the decision then this section will help you *evaluate* it, and assist you in understanding the environment your child (and you) are about to enter, as well as showing you how this compares with other options.

Which school *should* your child attend? The answer is not necessarily obvious (the school closest to you *may* or *may not* be the best option for your particular child). It is important to realise that this is not necessarily an inquiry that can be done in the abstract: it's about the best school *for your child.* And remember that, wherever possible, this is a decision that you should try and make with them. After all, if you choose the wrong school and have not consulted them throughout the process then you are risking a whole set of problems - from underachievement to difficulties with discipline. In short, making the decision alone represents a gamble for both of you.

Speaking to your child about the right school for them

1st Speak to your child! Find out what matters to them. It may not match up with what you are looking for in a school, but it is important that they are happy with the final decision

2nd Are they particularly interested in or good at a certain subject? If they enjoy sport or a specific subject like Art, Music, Languages or even Maths, you could consider how the school can help to develop these interests. Some state schools specialise in particular subjects like Technology, Sports or Art. You can find out more at http://www.standards.dfes.gov.uk/specialistschools/

3rd Visit potential schools with your child and talk to teachers or pupils in order to gain a suitable impression of the school. You can also check the facilities for their strengths in the areas your child is interested in.

The good news is there is data out there that may help you make your choice. Every year schools are subject to inspection and assessment. The body that carries this process out is called Ofsted (Office for Standards in Education, Children's Services and Skills). Ofsted inspectors arrive at schools having given them only short notice and, after observing the day-to-day activities of the school, issue a public report with their findings. To look for an Ofsted report for a certain school in your area visit the following site- http://www.ofsted.gov.uk/inspection-reports/find-inspection-report

It can be difficult to decide which school is best suited for your child because you want to make the best choice for not only their education, but their happiness. Sometimes the two appear to conflict. For example, your child may be accepted to a school with a good reputation; however they would prefer to go to a local secondary school with their primary school friends. Remember that the school with the best reputation is not necessarily the best school for your child. Here we have outlined types of schools and some of their basic pros and cons.

State Schools:

These include any school supported and funded by local authorities. They are all inspected by Ofsted and have to follow the National Curriculum. They can be roughly split into the following three groups although there are many specialist schools that you may want to research in more detail.

1. Comprehensive Schools:

These schools offer free education to children up to the age of 18. They are open to children of all abilities and have 'catchment areas,' which are the surrounding residential districts from which the school draws the majority of its students. If you are outside the catchment area and the school is very popular, your child may only be accepted if they already have siblings at the school.

Pros & Cons: comprehensive schools will have a wide mix of students, all of whom have come from different backgrounds and abilities. This can be great for your child as it will open them up to new experiences, ways of living and friendships. However, this may also be daunting to a child coming from a very small primary school with a close-knit group of friends. Will your child flourish in a bustling, extensive environment or would they be overwhelmed and therefore better suited to a smaller, more intimate school?

A number of your child's friends from primary school may be going to the same school, due to living in the same catchment area. This can potentially be a good thing, as they won't worry so much about making new friends at their new school. However, it can also present difficulties as it may affect their choice of school and prevent them going to a school that may be a better choice for them, academically. They may also rely too much on their old friends and therefore miss out on making new ones.

The teaching at comprehensive schools has to cater for all abilities, but don't think this means your child will be left behind or not be able to live up to their full potential. Comprehensive schools will normally place classes into 'sets' early on. These sets are dependent upon ability and aptitude and ensure that your child receives the most appropriate level of teaching. Some would say this could be detrimental for students who are able and for those who are less able, as the teachers have to cater for all levels of ability. However, there are always opportunities to move up or down sets, if their learning improves or if they appear to be struggling.

2. Grammar Schools:

These are run in much the same way as comprehensive schools, but entrance is based on academic ability. Your child will need to sit and pass the <u>11+ Exam or a particular entrance exam for the school </u>to receive a place. Often grammar schools are single sex so this is also something you will have to take into consideration when deciding with your child what school is best suited.

The 11+

The 11+ is an entrance examination taken by children in their final year of primary school. While they may be younger than eleven when they take the exam, the name refers to the age at which students will be when they begin the first year of secondary school. For students who sit the 11+, the exam is a key determinant in the school choices available to them. More specifically, students achieving a certain score are awarded places at a grammar school in the area. As discussed below, grammar schools are free to attend and the level of teaching is generally recognised as high. Therefore, the competition is strong as there are only limited places available.

When it was first administered, under the **Butler Education Act** back in the 1940s, the 11+ was a comprehensive test taken throughout the UK. Now, however, it is only administered by a handful of counties in England and Wales (while all children progressing to secondary school sit the test in Northern Ireland). For example, Kent and Essex still retain the 11+.

Substantively, the 11+ exam itself varies in the different counties which administer it. However, most cover **Maths** (including arithmetic and basic geometry**), English** (comprehension, reading and writing) and **Verbal Reasoning** (testing the child's ability to reason and think logically and to develop strategies for problem solving.

In the later 1990s there was a great deal of debate about the merits and demerits of the 11+ system (and the awarding of grammar school places to high performers). The debate has since lulled: the grammar school system, and the 11+ examination which determines whether students attain a place, looks like it is set to continue for the immediate future.

Pros & Cons: Grammar schools are known for encouraging academic ability. If your child does well with competition and challenge then a grammar school may be an ideal environment. However, this can work against some children who may be better suited to a non-competitive environment - where grades aren't the most important aspect of their learning.

Expected grades are likely to be higher at a grammar school, since the majority of classes will be required to work at a more advanced level. In the worst case scenario, this may result in a child who is weaker in a certain subject getting left behind, as the standard and expectation will be somewhat higher.

3. Faith Schools:

Faith Schools are usually run in the same way as other state schools. However, their faith status can be reflected in their curriculum, admissions criteria and staffing choices. For example, they may give preference to students based on their particular religious status.

Choosing a faith school is an important decision as the education provided will aim to mirror the values of the family's religion. Again, it is important to listen to and respect your child's views on this matter.

In some instances the status of a school as a 'faith school' is in fact nominal: it doesn't affect the curriculum for example. So the basic lesson is that with faith schools, as with other schools, you should do your research and be guided by both your judgment as to your child's best interests, and your child's judgment as to their own best interests.

4. Independent Schools:

These schools are not funded by local authorities: money to fund them comes from fees paid by parents or income from investments. They are monitored either by Ofsted or another regulatory body in the same way as state schools. They are also known as '**Private Schools'** and sometimes '**Public Schools'**. Obviously these contradictory names are quite confusing, but the most important thing to bear in mind is that these are both types of independently run schools that set up their own curriculum and admissions policies. The only real difference for our purposes are the names: public schools are those established before a certain date and tend to be more "traditional" or well-known (think Eton or Harrow).

You will have to pay tuition fees for these schools but some offer financial help in the way of bursaries and scholarships. More information and help can be found at the Independent Schools Council website http://www.isc.co.uk/ParentZone_Welcome.html

Pros & Cons: An independent school's main selling point is the flexibility they offer in terms of your child's learning. They can offer a much more tailored way of teaching since they do not have to follow the National Curriculum and generally have more to spend on resources for your child's education. You must balance this against the life experience your child might receive in a less sheltered setting. Also, independent schools may charge substantial fees. As a parent you may want to question whether money spent on school fees might be directed into other spheres to suitably develop your child's abilities and personality, for example getting your child a tutor or funding other creative or sporting interests outside of school.

Academies and Free Schools:

Academies

Academies are state-maintained independent schools: they are state-funded but operate outside of local authority control. One of the hallmarks of an academy is that it is set up with the help of an outside sponsor. This sponsor may be a university, but it could also be a business (Microsoft, Channel 4 and BT have all expressed wishes to be sponsors) or a faith group. Academies do not operate within the National Curriculum. Their only requirement is that the curriculum they do follow is 'broad and balanced.'

Free Schools

Free schools extend the idea of academies further. They set their own admission policies and have discretion to work towards a diverse curriculum. They are set up by groups of parents and teachers, charities or voluntary groups. As with academies, they will receive funding from the central government, but are not subjected to its overall control. The idea is a relatively new one, with the first 24 Free Schools opening in the UK in September 2011.

Pros & Cons: These types of school are relatively new and, as such, it is difficult to accurately gauge their pros and cons.

Having said that, the notion is not wholly untested - similar school structures exist, and are popular across the water in both directions. In the US, 'Charter Schools' are public sector schools that are not constrained by any National Curriculum, but still need to meet designated substantive standards of performance (as mandated in their own' Charter' at the stage of creation). In Sweden the model of a school that combines state support (financially) and yet relative autonomy (in terms of the subjects taught and approaches adopted) is well established and has been regarded as something of a success.

One of the touted benefits of the academy/free school model is that many will operate under 'extended hours' schedules meaning that the children can be dropped off earlier or picked up later from school. While the effects of this are likely to be more keenly felt in the primary school sector, this may be a benefit for parents with older children as well, especially when both parents work.

Mixed vs. Single Sex Schools:

Another thing you may wish to consider is whether you send your child to a mixed or single sex school. Single sex schools can often be faith schools or those that believe it is better for children academically to be separated. It can be a big factor in deciding a school, and there are many arguments **for** and **against**!

Single Sex

*The arguments **for** single sex schools are:*

- They stop children for being distracted from their studies, particularly teenagers (although there are some academic studies that disagree with this).
- They prevent children from becoming overly competitive with the opposite sex when studying together.
- They encourage children, particularly girls, to be less embarrassed about studying stereotypically 'male' subjects such as Maths /Science or stereotypically 'female' subjects such as Art/Home Economics/Music.
- Teaching can be better tailored to differences in ways of learning between girls and boys.

*The arguments **against** single sex schooling are:*

- They can create an artificial atmosphere that doesn't prepare students for the 'real world' of work or university after school.
- They can hinder students in developing social skills and natural relationships with the opposite sex.

Mixed Schools

Mixed schools of boys and girls together form the majority of schools across the country and your child may well have been in a mixed sex primary school and want to continue with a mixed secondary school.

*The arguments **for** mixed schools are:*

- Some studies show that boys perform better when in classes with girls who encourage them to act more responsibly. This of course may differ between schools.
- The school could be deemed have a more realistic environment, setting your child up for the world they are going to live in eventually.

*The arguments **against** mixed sex schools are:*

- Some research has shown that girls in particular, perform less well in a mixed sex environment, but again this will depend on the student in question and the school itself.
- Mixed schools may encourage students to become distracted by the opposite sex far more than in single sex schools.

For a more comprehensive (excuse the pun!) overview of the different schools on offer, and the different philosophies behind them visit the Department of Education's website at http://www.education.gov.uk/schools. For schools in England, you can also compare school performance, characteristics and spend per pupil data.

Coming to a decision

We must emphasise, these are simply introductions to the type of questions and considerations you face when making this important decision with your child. To get a more accurate idea of schools in your area you should do the following:

- Contact your Local Authority for information on schools near you. www.direct.gov.uk/en/DL1/Directories/Localcouncils/index.htm

- Send off for school prospectuses and read all the information through with your child
- Visit school open days and talk to teachers (this can be illuminating for you and your child as your child can gain a 'feeling' of how the school would be for them.)
- Look up the information held on a school's results or check their Ofsted inspection reports- these are often found in their prospectuses or websites, but if not try http://schoolsfinder.direct.gov.uk/
- If possible talk to other parents in your area about the types of schools available.

What if there are problems once my child starts school?

Don't panic: there is plenty of help and support available.

Moving schools: If the difficulties are insurmountable and you or your child feels they may need to move schools, this option is always available. You should seriously consider if the situation can be resolved before resorting to moving schools, as this could be difficult and disruptive for your child.

First, you must contact the school you wish your child to move to and find out if there are any places available and what the entry requirements are. After this they should be able to advise you on how to proceed.

The 13+

At 13 years it is possible to sit an entrance exam and move to a grammar school if there are available places, but these are very limited. Again, consider if this is the right thing for your child and if they would be suited to an academically minded environment and the disruptive change of friends and, possibly, pace.

If you agree on a choice of school then you should approach the new school to find details of if, and when, they are offering the exam for older students. This exam will usually be sat at the school itself. Not all grammar schools will have available places to accept new students into Year 9 so make sure first.

If you need more information on this then you can contact your Local Education Authority. Find your local office at http://www.dcsf.gov.uk/everychildmatters/ contacts/ or have a look at some of the various privately run websites which offer advice and information on the 11+ website (see for example http://www.elevenplusexams.co.uk).

Appealing against a school decision

Your child may not be awarded a place at the school which you feel is the best for them or equally which you feel they should rightly have been awarded. If your child falls into the former camp then there is limit to what can be done through a formal appeal process. If however, your child falls into the latter situation then you may want to consider the merits of making an appeal.

The details of how to make an appeal should be presented to you in the local authority's admission letter outlining your offer. There is almost certainly a deadline within which you will need to lodge the appeal. Presuming you are acting within this deadline, it is essential to be able to point to a substantive reason or ground of appeal. There may be mitigating circumstances such as your child was evidently unwell on the day of the exam, or you feel there is clear evidence of maladministration on the part of the LEA.

Beware, however, appeals are not an easy route of entry into the school of your choice. The appeal process is likely to be very stressful. For any appeal made you will need to provide ample supporting evidence and to make your case clearly and convincingly. The **Advisory Centre for Education** can provide you with independent advice on the nature and presentation of your appeal. Visit their website at http://www.ace-ed.org.uk/. However, you should note that the appeals process has been developed in order that you do not need any sort of professional advice, legal or otherwise.

The decision to appeal should be made in consultation with your child- it is worth remembering that it is primarily your child involved with the decision and it is not you that must attend the school you are trying to secure his or her place in. In short, the decision to appeal should not be a rash one and it should not be your decision alone.

2. LOOKING AFTER YOUR CHILD'S EDUCATIONAL NEEDS

Once your child moves to secondary school, they may need your help to adjust to the new workload and differences in teaching methods and subjects. Don't panic! You don't need to know everything about plant biology or be able to do quadratic equations; you just need to provide your child with a good working environment and some healthy advice and care.

Tips to motivate your child:

- Encourage them to try different <u>methods of learning</u>. They may find that making notes from a book is enough, but if that's a bit too boring they could also try different revision websites, which have already been mentioned in the student section, or make mind maps or posters when revising. There is a whole section on this later in the book.
- Encourage them to read for fun, not just for school. If they are interested in reading and writing at home it will make it easier and more enjoyable when they have to do the same at school.
- If they have a goal in life, to be a doctor, a teacher, or even an astronaut, then encourage them and let them know how to achieve this through their education.
- Encourage them to take regular, short breaks. Whether your child works for 6 hours straight or gets bored after half an hour, they all **need a break** to be more productive and generally happier.
- Encourage them to be creative if they are struggling to remember facts and figures. Suggest drawing a poster of what they've been learning as an extra way to reinforce what they need to remember.
- It's OK to spot that your child is weak in a certain subject area, but don't force Maths on them because you are good at Maths. Your child is not you; don't try and make them be.

A Good Study Area:

It is very important for your child to have a place with the right equipment and space in which to study. If their room is too cluttered or has too many temptations to stop working then maybe a quiet spot elsewhere in the house will help. Make sure there is good light, enough space for all their books and equipment, and that they have regular breaks.

Your child's bedroom should be a haven- somewhere they can work effectively but also somewhere they can relax. We strongly encourage parents to forbid the presence of computers and televisions in children's bedrooms. Time and time again we have seen the deleterious effect that each can have. When it comes to televisions, children will often sleep with the television on, which disrupts sleep and can leave them unable to fully concentrate the next day. There is also the risk that they will be exposed to content you simply do not think is appropriate. With computers (whether it be a PC or other home computer or a console like a PlayStation) we see the negative effect that 'gaming' has on their concentration and even their ability to interact with other children and parents in the real world. For every soar in motor reflexes that follow from your child's playing of a computer game there is a corresponding dive in attention span.

There is no need to be overly dramatic here. Televisions and computers, particularly those that provide access to the Internet, are a remarkably valuable portal to the outside world - a fantastic prism that can open their eyes to a range of insights and places if used appropriately. Your child will need a computer in particular to conduct research for their homework, to more generally educate themselves and to keep in touch with friends. You would be doing wrong to deny them access to this. As such, the maxim 'everything in moderation' holds well here. The point we are trying to emphasise is that playing the role of moderator is nearly impossible when there is a bedroom door that can shut you out. Ensure televisions and computers are housed in a communal spot where your child can freely access them, but where you are able to observe and appropriately regulate their use.

Making Revision Plans:

We have already covered revision timetables in the student section of this book but your child may need a little help and encouragement to make a realistic and helpful plan. How can you help?

- Double check with them when and where any exams are, or when homework is due in, so that everything gets done on time.
- Don't push them or allow them to try to do too much. More than 2 or 3 subjects a night can be a little excessive.
- Suggest they start with their least favourite subject and finish with their favourite to make sure they spend enough time on each and to keep them motivated.
- Help them make diagrams, flash cards or mind maps as suggested in the student section to help them revise in a variety of different ways

TOP TIPS:

If you are feeling a little rusty yourself (and who can remember how to do long division anymore?) then you could always take a refresher course in anything from Maths and English to IT and Computing. The government offers free DVD's to help you, so that you can help your child.

hhttp://www.direct.gov.uk/em/EducationAndLearning/AdultLearning/ImprovingYourSkills/index.htm

If things go wrong:

If your child is having problems with exams or tests at school they will need your encouragement. Whether it is because they are struggling with the subject or because they do not enjoy it. They need to be reminded of the importance of exams BUT at the same time, keep it in perspective for them. Failing one exam isn't the end of the world, and at school there will be plenty of opportunities to make up for missed work or poor results.

Tutoring Options:

If your child is struggling with certain subjects, that you can't realistically help them with, a tutor is a good option. This doesn't have to be expensive or time consuming. Even an hour a week can really help your child catch up if they are behind or just to get to grips with a difficult subject.

Before looking for a private tutor it is worth checking with your child's school as they may have free study sessions available at lunchtime or after school. If this is not possible there are many ways of finding a good, reliable tutor. Teachers at the school may offer private tuition, or friends of your child may recommend a tutor.

Some tutors will recommend having the session away from home, either at school or at their house or a library as this helps your child to work in a place they don't associate with playing, eating or anything not work related. This tip can help when your child needs to work alone on homework or revision too.

Learning Difficulties:

If you are concerned that your child may have specific learning difficulties and are unsure what to do then help is at hand, or if you are aware of your child's learning difficulties but are unsure of your choices, you should know that there *is* support out there.

If you suspect that your child may have learning difficulties, the first person to talk to would be the child's teacher, as they should already have a good idea of how your child is getting on. If need be they can refer you to the school's '**Special Educational Needs Co-ordinator**' who are specially trained to carry out assessments in order to determine what the problem may be.

For children with a statement of special educational needs it is the job of the local council's '**Special Educational Needs Team**' to talk with parents and schools to agree on a suitable programme for your child. This process should ideally start as soon as possible in the child's academic journey. Early detection is always best.

The majority of children will transfer from primary school to a mainstream state secondary school with little difficulties, but there is also the option of a special school designed to cater more effectively for the needs of certain children. If you think your child may benefit from a special school you should contact your Local Education Authority.

Looking after your child's health needs:

We discuss healthy eating in the student section of this book, and hopefully your child will soon understand the value of eating well! Children's diets can have a huge effect on their school performance and general wellbeing. You can make sure they are feeling at their best on the longer school day by giving them a balanced diet.

Breakfast is vitally important for supplying energy throughout the day. Don't let your child skip breakfast, even if it's only a slice of toast (preferably wholemeal bread). Some schools have recognised how difficult it is to teach children suffering from low energy supplies and they now provide breakfast clubs for the children.

Unfortunately the cafeterias in some schools still offer poor healthy eating options. Packed lunches are a great way of making sure your child doesn't have chips for lunch every day and will help ensure they get the high energy, healthy foods needed to maintain concentration.

3. LOOKING AFTER YOUR CHILD'S SOCIAL NEEDS

How much freedom is too much?

We've all heard our parents say it to us -"Things weren't like this in my day." It's true, times change and therefore your experience of secondary school may be very different from what your child will experience in the coming years. It can be difficult to know how much independence to give them and how strict you should be, especially if they are telling you that their friends' parents let them stay up past midnight and watch whatever they want.

The best rule of thumb is essentially whatever feels right to you, but only *after* you have thought about the situation as objectively as possible. That is to say, while you know your child best and your instinct can be useful, your gut feelings will not always be in your child's best interests. Accept that things are different from when you were growing up. Listen to your child's needs. Employ common sense and think about the extent of freedom they need *dispassionately*. Some parents overburden their children with restrictive rules because they know they could not live with themselves if anything went wrong, serious or not. Driven by anxiety, these parents are living their children's lives for them. They are quashing choice and therefore diluting that great possibility of learning from mistakes made. Try not to be that parent- it benefits nobody.

1. Money

You will probably be asked for more money for school lunches or snacks. It's great for children to learn the importance of money. If you feel they are ready you may want to give them money for the week rather than each day to let them learn how to budget. If you are unsure how much to give, get a rough idea of food prices at school or what other parents give their children (ask the parents themselves if possible).

2. Rules

Your child will probably expect more freedom in their social and home life as they mature. They may ask to be allowed to stay out later on school nights or weekends or stay up to watch a favourite TV show that 'everyone else' watches. Again, you must remember that they have to adjust to a new school and new friends and will need a bit more freedom to enjoy this. However, that does not mean letting them have everything they ask for! Structure and rules still play a key part in your child's education and wellbeing at school and at home. Actually, most children expect reasonable boundaries and rules- not to provide these as a parent is a big mistake. Be reasonable.

3. Friends

Your child will be making all kinds of new friends. Some friendships may last; some may just drift apart over time. Whatever happens, it is important that your child knows they can still talk to you. It is important to support them as much as possible. Their friends will probably live further away than at primary school, so you may be expected to give them lifts to a friend's house occasionally. It's important you support your child in this way.

4. The Internet

The Internet is the greatest academic resource your child will ever have access to. Services such as **Wikipedia** (an online user generated encyclopaedia) and **Google Books** (which stores millions of books from across the world that can be freely accessed online), have revolutionised the way children learn and the paths through which they conduct academic research. You should be cautious, but not scared, of the fact that your child **will** spend time on the Internet, researching information or generally 'hanging out'. With sufficient vigilance the Internet can be a safe and rewarding resource, which contributes to your child's academic and personal growth.

This book draws your child's attention to some of the dangers they may face online in the student section. Try yourself to be aware of these dangers and you can act as a source of monitoring and guidance. But be aware that you will need to both _warn and trust_ your child, since you simply cannot stand and watch over their shoulder, every moment they are online. One of the most controversial areas of Internet use among young people is the use of social networks.

5. Social Networking

Social networks are online communities built around users with similar interests or prior social connections. Social networks are a part of most young people's lives. Officially, to use '**Facebook**'- the most popular network- you must be at least 13 years old, but this has not stopped many younger students setting up their own accounts with false dates of birth. In fact, the chances are that your child is already using the Internet and various chatting facilities or social networking sites such as '**Facebook**,' '**MySpace**' or '**Twitter**.' The second half of this book, which is aimed at your child, has a section outlining the various risks associated with the use of these sites and the Internet more generally.

As a parent you need to know that the use of these sites presents both opportunities and threats. They are a great way for your child to develop friendships they already have at secondary school, or to ensure that they keep in contact with good friends from primary school once they move onto secondary school. Your child may also use these sites to keep in contact with family members who live further away. These uses are perfectly safe and they are an essential part of your child's development and their general social welfare.

However, there are also threats from using such sites. On the one hand, these sites are to some extent 'closed' - your child must give permission for a new 'friend' to have access to their data and personal details, and so they are safer than traditional 'chatrooms', where anonymous users can contact your child and masquerade as anybody. On the other hand, there are still serious concerns about the sort of material your child could be exposed to. Crucially, there are also considerable privacy concerns relating to the fact that these sites encourage the sharing of personal information such as your child's hometown, current location and family pictures. You should ensure your child has set **strict privacy controls** to guard against outside interferences and meddling with their private lives.

It is also important to make your child aware of the difficulties they could get into on social networking sites. Some children have been known to use these sites to bully other students. Schools draw little distinction between activity occurring online _during_ school hours, and _after_. Online harassment and bullying, or the posting of explicit or otherwise inappropriate material on the Internet is treated very seriously by schools and can lead to pupils being suspended or excluded. It is very important therefore, to make sure your child knows not to write any comments which may be considered upsetting, or equally to put up with any threats or bullying from other people.

If you are really worried about the amount of time that your child is using on these sites and on the Internet more generally, you can set up **parental controls** on the computer and warn them about chatting online to people they don't know. If you are concerned that they may not be focusing on their schoolwork enough then **set time limits** for Internet usage or reward them with Internet time only after they finish their homework.

4. LOOKING AFTER YOUR CHILD'S EMOTIONAL NEEDS

Emotional Intelligence

This is a big one. In our opinion its importance can hardly be exaggerated. As a parent you cannot, and quite simply must not, overlook the significance of your child's emotional intelligence.

Emotional intelligence is a term your child could go through their whole school life without hearing. The absence of a dedicated and strategic approach to dealing with emotional intelligence in our formal secondary education system is one of its biggest failings. Leadership here has to come from the top, and not enough decision makers in government or schools themselves have grasped that their duty is to provide a system which not only prepares children academically for the world they are to enter (and in time run!) but also that they must create happy, healthy, rounded young men and women too.

In the shadow of schools' failures, parents fare little better. Largely their obstacle is simply a lack of awareness about what the concept means, and how it can be engaged and refined. Many different definitions of emotional intelligence exist but in essence it refers to a person's ability to understand their own feelings and emotions. Of course, through this understanding comes the ability to understand others- to empathise with, to care for and to understand the people we share our lives with. A child with strong emotional intelligence is likely to be successful in school, maintaining healthy relationships with teachers and students alike. But more importantly they are likely to be a happy, healthy person with self-confidence and an optimistic take on life.

Daniel Goleman's numerous, and consistently insightful, books on the matter of emotional intelligence provide a once controversial but now widely accepted argument that emotional intelligence is more accurate in predicting the success and happiness of a person's life far more than any other single thing- including socio-economic background and IQ. Your child would, then, do well to come to understand the concept and seek to develop their emotional intelligence. You, as a parent, would do wrong not to help them with this.

In our years of experience teaching children (and being children ourselves) we have time and time again seen that a child with poor emotional intelligence may be prone to anger or poor behaviour. Often this is the result of frustration at not being able to understand the reason for the constant trials and troubles they face at this age; for this is indeed an age marked by considerable change. New friendships groups, new expectations, puberty- it can be overwhelming trying to understand how to react to this when your sense of identity is slight and you cannot understand the reasons you feel the way you do.

Encourage your child to be reflective and thoughtful about the way they are feeling. Guide them through a process of understanding their emotions. If they are sad- don't try simply to cheer them up with a trip to the cinema, or a shopping spree. Speak with them about their feelings: try to make them understand the reasons they are feeling that way. Empower your child to alter their emotions by encouraging them to talk about those emotions and trace their feelings back to events that triggered them.

Allow them to realise how the emotions they feel affect their thoughts and their behaviour. Show them that they can overcome impulsive behaviour (tantrums, aggression, tears before bedtime, bad behaviour in school) by understanding the emotions that underpin that sort of action.

Point out to them the importance of non-verbal communication. Persuade them that they should pay attention to people's eye contact, their tone of voice, their posture and their use of gesture. The more your child looks at this in others, the more they will be aware of their own.

Encourage your child to be aware of their place in a wider system. They are one student- one of many. Allow them to realise that there are power dynamics in every social situation and that they can reinforce or adjust them. An emotionally intelligent child is one that understands the needs and concerns of others in a social situation, and often has the strength to speak up in defence of those who need it. They are able to understand the true character of the relationships they have with people- with friends, with teachers, with their parents- and so better able to manage them and maintain those relationships.

Be patient. Developing emotional awareness is one of the hardest things we can do. But it can be done. Expose your child to a rich array of sources that cultivate their propensity to reflect. Take them to the theatre. Take them to see films that they might otherwise not choose to see. Suggest books for them to read. Then talk about these things with them. "How did they make you feel?"

Ask them about their friends. And ask them about their friends' relationships with one another. Encourage them to be the detective in their group- always questioning and considering. But remember that being patient means you cannot force anything on them, or expect them to understand the value of what you are trying to develop in them right away.

Challenge them, but always do so constructively. Challenging means asking them to explain their gut reactions to things. If they hated a book you suggest they read, ask them why. What did it make them feel? How would they prefer to feel? If they have an argument with a friend, ask them how that felt and not simply what happened.

Encourage your child to be compassionate. Ask them to imagine the world through someone else's eyes. How would it feel to walk a day in their friend's boots? Or their teachers? Or yours?

Point out to them the value of using humour to deal with some of the challenges they face. Show them how trivial; even funny some problems can seem when you remove yourself from the picture. Show humour yourself.

Remind them that conflict is inevitable- not everyone they meet will like them; they will not like everyone they meet. And remember you too, as parent and child, will have your moments of conflict. Have the emotional intelligence to see this for what it is. It is part of your child's development: part of their questioning of the old roles you both once took. Do not overplay the significance of your child's apparent disrespect for a curfew or budget you set, or a commitment you required. If you anticipate and understand that sporadic conflict between parents and young adults of this age is inevitable, then when it comes to emotional intelligence your child's best teacher will be you.

You should be patient because this patience will be a reflection of your own emotional intelligence. But more importantly by far, you should be patient because it takes time to grow an asset. And you are helping to grow one of the greatest assets your child will ever own- the ability to ask who they really are, and the ability to find comfort in the answer.

Stillness

The observation or practice of stillness and meditation is something that is slowly (in our view much too slowly) creeping into the education system in the UK.

What do we even mean by 'stillness'? We mean the deliberate attempt to create a designated time and space in which to embrace 'quiet' and the pursuit of a feeling of inner calmness or peace. When we talk about 'stillness' we are describing the effort to clear the mind- to empty it of the rubbish that may have accumulated there during that day or week.

Needless to say, this is not something that you are going to find dominating the narrative of governmental educational policy. Nevertheless, some schools in the UK now have daily or weekly 15-minute slots of 'stillness time'. This is not prayer time. It is quiet thinking time, or ideally, a time to forget one's thoughts and just focus on one's breathing. It should be emphasised that there is nothing mystical or religious about this. It is about reclaiming the inner peace that we all can enjoy, but seldom do.

It's also about harnessing and channelling our energies. Many of us have seen this channelling if we have ever observed the 10-second pause before a David Beckham free kick or a Jonny Wilkinson drop-goal, or before an Olympic medal winning gymnastics performance. But the truth is that each and every one of us can benefit from an introduction to stillness. Your child is no exception. It will calm them, improve their concentration and may prove their one chance at relaxation in an otherwise frenetic day. Let's not forget that the likelihood is that your child faces more distractions, more demands on their time, than you ever did. In a world of ever-present, always plugged in technology- PlayStations, the Internet, social networking, televisions- it is harder than you think for your child to find time to simply switch-off. The reality is that academic and social expectations, too, are likely to be greater for your child now than they were for you. We see children run from classrooms to after-school clubs to tuition classes in order to fulfil the expectations of parents, teachers and a government that now expects more of its young people than ever in the past. These expectations persist, if not inflate, with time. Secondary school admission can be fierce and competitive, but it is ballet compared with the bar-brawl that is university admission. In short, your child will be told over and over that they have to work very hard, yet still maintain all manner of extra-curricular activities in order to 'keep up with the pack' and be successful as they get older. In short we are demanding extraordinary things of our children. We are asking them to sprint along the circus high wire of life when we as children could simply tip toe. Show your child the value of stillness in their life and you could protect them from a fall: it's something they will be very thankful for.

Just don't expect the thanks to start straight away. When you begin to talk about stillness they may think this is the single silliest idea you have every come up with. But our experience has shown us that in time they will come to appreciate it.

How to begin? First of all, ensure your child has a space they can truly relax in. Ask yourself whether their bedroom is a relaxing place. If the last decoration in there was when they were six years old then chances are the 'My Little Pony' wallpaper needs to go. Ensure their bedroom is not cluttered. Go out to the local shops or jump online and buy them a lava lamp or another calming light of some sort. Their room is somewhere they must be comfortable spending time- whether it is for relaxing or doing homework. (Note that we would strongly encourage you to remove any televisions or computers from their bedrooms. See the section on 'Looking After Your Child's Educational Needs' for more information).

Then, introduce them to the idea of suspending their thoughts- the idea of doing *nothing but being*. To begin with it might help to give them something to focus on as a distraction from normal day-to-day thought. Put some slow looping music on- something unobtrusive like a simple, repetitive piano piece and ask them to focus on the music, and the music alone. They should be trying not to conjure up any thoughts or use their imagination in any way. It is remarkably hard to do and your child will likely resist at first. The mind wants to be busy; it is at its most comfortable when a flood of thoughts flows through it. But stick with it. Its fine for them to laugh at the situation at first, and it's probably healthy for you to do the same. But after a while things will improve. The periods of stillness will become longer. Eventually you can remove the music and come to realise the value of creating some time apart from the bustle of the real world, even just a few minutes, to be fully relaxed: to do and think nothing.

As well as improving your child's ability to concentrate in class (and to complete tasks like homework with minimal distraction and therefore in minimal time), introducing stillness to their life will help them reclaim a sense of peace and calm which will make them happier.

Nothing we have said here is about you trying to dampen the fire within your child. Their energy is a remarkable thing - a precious, precious gift that most adults are in awe of. It's a terrible shame to see parents try and subdue their children. This is never about that. Instead it's about showing them that it is possible to switch off; and that it is absolutely OK to do that. It's about allowing them to come to terms with themselves. It is about developing their emotional intelligence and allowing them to understand their emotions and thoughts by stepping outside of them, even for a brief few minutes. Try introducing this to your child's life. Wait patiently. Now, notice how they smile more.

5. DEAR MARIA/ FAQs

As you have seen, the transfer to secondary school can be a difficult and challenging time for parents as well as children.

Here are some of the most frequent concerns that parents have at this time:

> *Dear Maria,*
>
> *My child is transferring to secondary school soon and we are concerned that the new school will be unaware of his difficulties with reading. How much information does the new school have about our child?*

Maria says:

It is in the interest of everyone that the transfer goes as smoothly as possible. Therefore the feeder school will almost certainly have provided the secondary school with a surprising amount of detailed information about the child's strengths and areas of concern, much of this information having been received from SATs and other formal tests. A personal profile of your child will also be provided in order for the secondary school to best meet the needs of the individual. Many secondary schools adopt a 'clean slate' approach to get the very best out of each student.

> *Dear Maria,*
>
> *My child is concerned that she will be put into a tutor group or classes with no one she knows. How are the groups organised?*

Maria says:

It is important for your child to meet new people and make new friends, however the school is also aware that your child must feel comfortable in their new surroundings, therefore the tutor group will attempt to accommodate a small number of friends from the same school. The class groups are often formed on the basis of ability, either as shown from the primary school input or an assessment test may be set in Maths or English when the child starts their secondary school. These 'sets' are transitory and your child can move up or down as the year progresses, depending on their efforts and abilities. Each school will have a particular policy on this matter.

Dear Maria

How will I know how my child has settled in and if they are coping with the range of different subjects?

Maria says:

Obviously your child needs some time to settle down and learn the new systems and ways of operating in their new school. The first half-term is a 'settling down' period where your child will tackle a range of new subjects and meet their new teachers. Often there will be a 'meet the tutor' evening in the first few weeks which enables you to personally talk to your child's first point of contact in the school.

Subject teachers are usually met at the first 'parents evening' and a brief written report may have been provided prior to this which will supply you with a level of attainment (National Curriculum level 4 to level 5 and an effort grade).

Dear Maria

My child does not seem to be very happy at his new secondary school and he is now complaining of being unwell in the morning in order to stay at home. I suspect he may be getting bullied. What should I do?

Maria says:

Bullying in school is taken very seriously. Do not hesitate to speak to the school about your concerns. Your child's tutor is usually the first point of contact, but equally the Head of Year may be the person especially equipped to deal with the issue of bullying. A sympathetic hearing will be given and the matter should be dealt with swiftly.

> *Dear Maria,*
>
> *My child is getting a lot of homework, from a range of new subjects, and he keeps asking me to help him with it. How much help should I realistically be giving him?*

Maria says:

There is no hard and fast rule here, but generally teachers do expect the student to make some attempt on their own at completing their homework. They would prefer to see the child's own efforts, all be it not perfect, than a fantastic piece of work completed by the parents!

Some children do need a bit more support, depending on their academic skills, but do be wary of doing the work for them- this helps no-one, and gives a false impression to the teacher who may assume the child does not need extra reinforcement in a particular area of work. Remind your child to ask the teacher for help if they do not understand what they are being asked to do

.

> *Dear Maria,*
>
> *We do not feel that the secondary school our child attends is the right one for her? What choices do we have?*

Maria says:

It is always important to give your child time to adapt to a new school. It is challenging and can sometimes appear overwhelming for a child initially. However, most children do settle down after the first term. If your child is still unhappy, then it is important to talk to the school and try and resolve any apparent difficulties. If after trying to work things out the school is really not the right one for your child, then explore which other schools may be more suitable. See the sections in this book on exactly that topic.

6. WHAT DO YOU WANT FOR YOUR CHILD?

Whatever you want your child to be they will be. Even if they don't initially share your passion to be a doctor, a lawyer, an engineer, a singer, an actor; it is inevitable that eventually they will realise your wisdom, come round to your viewpoint and share your ambitions. If you are tenacious and pushy enough you can ensure that the long-held dreams you have for your child will become their own dreams for themselves. More than that, you will both take great joy in seeing those dreams come true. For this, they will thank you forever.

We hope that this sounds as ridiculous for you to read as it felt for us to write. This account is very far from the truth but unfortunately our experience has shown us that many parents in fact believe some version of this nonsense and that it can be the source of much conflict, sooner or later, between parents and children. The reality is far more nuanced than this. Your child needs and wants your help with the transition they are going through, and more generally with determining the course and character of their life, but they also must make their own decisions, find their own path and develop their own style. This is common sense. In fact, in many ways, the intention of this book is to revitalise the common sense parents abandon when it comes to their own children.

Search for and indulge the strengths your child shows, whatever they are. It is entirely possible that they may not be academically strong. But if your child adheres to some of the tips in this book- altering the way they approach their homework, the way they structure their learning and revision for exams and how they approach and manage their relationships with teachers then they are very likely to comfortably hurdle the academic thresholds set by schools and government. And even if they do not, there is nothing to be gained by erroneously convincing your child that this is all that matters. That is why it is so important not to stifle the debate about what it is important to be 'good at'. Your child's performance in Maths and Science will not determine the course of their life if you help to cultivate other strengths in them - their emotional intelligence and their soft skills like negotiation and active listening, all discussed in this book. We believe that there is no such thing as a lazy child; just one that has not found, or been given, the right motivation. Be a positive source of motivation and inspiration if you can. If your child likes reading stories, encourage them to write a short one of their own. If they like listening to music, encourage them to play an instrument. If they like scribbling on paper, encourage them to draw.

While it is true that getting underway with secondary school represents the start of a crucial developmental phase in your child's life and a great opportunity to establish ways of working, thinking and living that will serve them well throughout their lives, it is also imperative to remember that they are still very young. They are beginning secondary school, not securing their Ph.D. At this stage the stakes are seldom so high that what seems hopeless cannot be turned into success. Embrace the fact that for both child and parent, there are many mistakes to be made and many frustrations to endure.

Seek always to recall one thing. Education is self-discovery. It is not, and should never be, *simply* about acquiring knowledge. The educated young man or woman is not someone who has cured an informational deficit. They are someone who has produced an insatiable itch, an unquenchable thirst: the persisting need to find out more about themselves, the world they live in, and the people they share it with. Seen in this way, education is about allowing children to uncover and actualise their own potential. As a parent you can help them do this but, by definition, you cannot do this for them. Their own dreams are what they will do best living. So, do as you did many, many years ago when you helped your child begin to walk. Step back and accept that they may stumble a little at first- you shouldn't expect anything different and you will be there to catch them if the fall would truly be too painful. But, our feeling is that if you both follow the principles outlined in this book then your child will walk tall very soon. Don't forget to clap when they do.

STUDENT SECTION

INTRODUCTION

Ok it's true, preparing for secondary school can seem scary! New buildings, new subjects, new teachers, and making new friends – it is all new!

But here is a little secret. Just because it is new, doesn't mean it has to be daunting. With the right advice, preparation and attitude it can be fun. It can be exciting. It can be interesting. It could be the best years of your life.

This book is crammed with advice from secondary school teachers and tips and stories from students. You can learn from their experiences. It will show you what to expect from a typical school day, how to prepare for your very first day and more generally HOW TO GET THE MOST OUT OF SECONDARY SCHOOL through a range of study techniques.

It will show you how to organise your time so that you can do all the homework and exam revision you need and still have time for extra-curricular activities like joining a sports team or debating society or chess club. Or perhaps all three…

TRUE STORY:

'My first weeks at school were such a blur, making new friends, learning about my new school, I don't feel like I even did any studying but I'm sure I did! The best thing for me was all the new things you could try. Not just school subjects, although I love learning to speak French, but also all the sports and having so many people to play them with. It's even better than primary school!'

Tom (12)

After reading this book you will realise that preparing for secondary school isn't scary at all. The best way to read this book is to read only one or two chapters at any one sitting. That way you will have time to properly think about the advice given - be it someone's true story about their own experiences, or the advice of us as authors. Take time to try and complete the little quizzes and games throughout the book. These will not only teach you incredibly important things (like how you, personally, learn best), they will also make the book feel like it belongs to *you*. That's the most important thing because, never forget, everything within the covers of this book is written for *your benefit*. Moving to secondary school will be a happier, more successful experience if you don't forget that.

To get you started, try this exercise…

DRAW YOUR NEW SCHOOL BADGE:

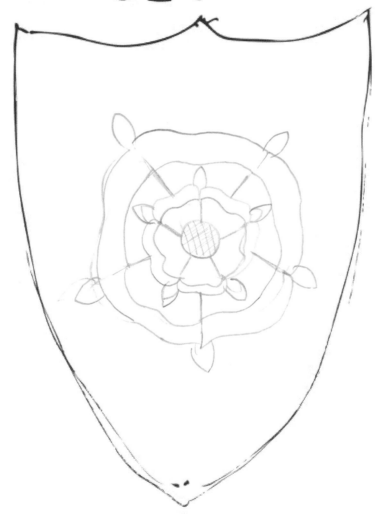

What is your school motto? Not for Our ....

What does it mean? ....

1. WHEEL OF CHANGE

How are you feeling?

It may seem like your whole world is changing! It's ok to feel a little disrupted and confused about all these changes. Just remember that everyone has to go through this change- you aren't alone.

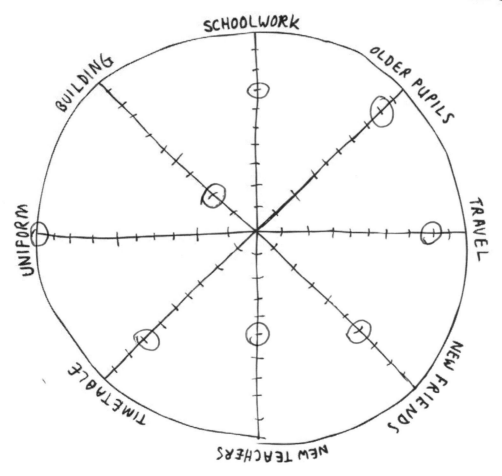

18.05.21

- ✓ On a Scale of 1-10 (1 – least/10 – most) mark on the wheel how concerned you are about the move to secondary school. (10 = centre of the wheel, 1 = outside of the wheel.)

- ✓ You should review this wheel after 6 Months at secondary school – you might be surprised that what you thought was a cause for concern really shouldn't have been.

Make a list of some of the things you are looking forward to and those that you are concerned about.

I am really looking forward to...

- More subjects/clubs.
- Good friends.
- Learning
- Formal uniform
- Freedom : Choose what I want to ~~keep~~ eat.

I am concerned about...

- Competition (sort of)
- Getting lost.
- Wearing coat inside by accident

TOP TIPS:

When you've finished this book why not look back and see how many concerns you can cross out and how many new things you can add to your 'looking forward to' section.

2. PREPARING FOR THE FIRST DAY

School Uniform

All schools will have a set uniform for all the younger years (once you reach the sixth form you may even be able to wear your own clothes). Your new school will send you a **uniform list** to get ready for your first day. Some schools will be more flexible and relaxed with their uniform, e.g. trousers and a shirt for boys and skirt or trousers for girls. Your new school might be stricter with uniform and it's a good idea to make sure you have all the right things for your first day. If you're worried about looking silly, just have a look at what students already wear at your new school on an open day or maybe just walking past. You'll soon see they all look more or less the same in their uniforms.

Choosing a Bag:

Choosing a good school bag is really important. It needs to be big enough to hold the books you need (as well as any PE kit or packed lunch you might have). It is also important that it provides enough support for your back otherwise it could give you backache or bad posture, not what you need on your longer school day!

There are three main types of bags

1. *Backpack (also called a rucksack:)* This has two straps that go over the shoulders (some have just one strap worn over the chest) and provide great support. These are a great all round bags and are the most popular for those starting secondary school.
2. *Shoulder-bag or Record-bag:* These are worn over just one shoulder. They are generally smaller than backpacks and provide less support for the back. They can be good for carrying PE kit though.
3. *Briefcase or satchel:* Very few students use briefcases or satchels anymore. They are often heavy, provide no back support and can't be washed (not great for carrying stinky trainers after football or hockey).

What to Pack: It's important to know what to pack for your first day. There are some essential things and some optional things.

ESSENTIAL (you would be silly not to pack these)

- ✓ Any textbooks you have been advised to buy before school starts (normally schools will hand out textbooks on the first few days)
- ✓ Exercise books or a large pad of A4 paper. The school will probably give you exercise books for each subject but if you want something to write notes in on the first day this is a good idea
- ✓ A pencil case containing pencils, a good pen for writing with (can be a biro or fountain pen and must be either blue or black ink), a spare pen in case your other one breaks or gets lost, a pencil sharpener, colouring pencils (for geography and for visual presentations), a rubber and a 30cm ruler
- ✓ A calculator for Maths, preferably a scientific one so you can use it all through your GCSEs

OPTIONAL (you can pack these or not, it won't make you more or less silly)

- ✓ A packed lunch
- ✓ PE kit if you need it
- ✓ Trainers or comfortable shoes to play football or netball in at break time (check your school allows you to change your shoes for this, and always remember to change back for lessons)
- ✓ Maths equipment such as a compass and protractor, but your teachers will be able to advise you on this

TOP TIPS:

ALWAYS, ALWAYS, ALWAYS pack your bag the night before! This is a key part of being organised and ensures you don't forget anything important like your homework.

3. GETTING TO SCHOOL

Deciding how to get to school is important; therefore you need to talk to your parents about this. If your new school is very far away then you may have no option but to take the arranged school bus. Don't worry too much about this journey. Within a few days you will know everyone on the bus and going to school and coming back will probably be the highlight of your day. If your secondary school is a little closer then you will have more options. Let's consider some of these.

Walking - This is a great way to get to school if you don't have too far to go. If you know there is someone who lives near you who is going to the same school as you then you can arrange to walk to school on your first day with them. If you aren't sure then walk to school with an older brother or sister (or your Mum or Dad) on the first day. You are likely to meet someone at school who you can walk with in the future.

Going by bike - You may wish to ride to school. Nearly all schools have a bike shed where you can lock up your bike (good bike locks are available from Halfords or Argos and are essential if you are going to ride to school). For safety reasons, make sure you wear a helmet and some bright reflective clothing if you are going to be riding in the winter when it can be dark in the mornings and evenings. You may want to undertake a course in bike riding to be absolutely sure that you can ride in any conditions and still remain safe. Try this website for fun and useful bike riding training - http://www.bikeability.org.uk/

Public bus or train - If you want to travel by public bus then it can be cheaper to buy weekly tickets. If your new school hasn't already provided you with the information, you should contact your local council about getting a student pass, which will entitle you to concessions (until you are over 16). For train travel, weekly tickets will be cheaper and by applying for a student railcard you will get one-third off of normal prices. Go into your local train station for information.

Taking Care - Whatever form of travel you decide on, you must always have safety as your number one consideration. If you are walking or cycling try and travel in a small group and never take shortcuts if they might put you in danger. Remember that if you are staying late at school for sport or after-school clubs you may be travelling home later than normal. Always inform your parents about this and keep in touch with them via your mobile.

Things you should ideally try and do by the time you arrive on day one:

- ✓ Checked that you know both the school address and that you know how you will get there, and how long it will take – you don't want to be late on your first day.
- ✓ Checked that you have all the necessary parts of the uniform.
- ✓ Make a file in which you put all the different letters that your school have sent you and any details of public transport, such as bus times.
- ✓ Buy a bag, pencil case, pens, pencils, rulers etc.
- ✓ Buy a **personal organiser** that you plan your life in. You will soon be able to use this to record your homework or write down anything that the teacher says in the lesson that may be of use. You can also use it to check which homework you have to do that night so that you bring home the right books. Your school will also give you a homework diary, but you may find it easier to have everything in one place.

4. THE FIRST DAY

It is natural to be concerned about your first day at secondary school. Most people are fearful that they won't make any friends. This can be especially worrying if you are not going to secondary school with people you know from primary school. The idea of trying to make new friends may seem daunting. What you will find is that everyone is eager to be friendly to one another! Your teacher is likely to ask you to say a few words about yourself, such as your name, where you live and what you like to do in your spare time. This will give you a chance to get to know everyone in your class.

TRUE STORY:

When I first moved to my new school there were some people in my form that were really loud and sounded so confident, like they knew everything. I was too nervous to talk to them until I had to sit next to one of them in Maths. I found out we were both scared about making friends, we just dealt with it in different ways. She was loud to make her seem confident. I stayed quiet to make it seem like I knew what was going on! We're best friends now!

Sarah (12)

What to Expect
Many things about secondary school are likely to be just the same as you are used to at primary school. There will be school assemblies, and you will have lessons in English and Maths. Also, you will probably still have one main group of friends with whom you spend

most of your free time- that is breaks and eating your lunch. Maybe you are even going to secondary school with some people you already know. However, the most important link between secondary and primary school is that **you will be there to learn new things.**

But there will be some big differences too…

THE BIG THREE!

1: First, you will be the youngest year students at the school. This will be a big change as previously you have been used to being the oldest students at your primary school. Some of you might even have had responsibility over other students, if you were prefects or House Captains. You will no longer be the 'top dog' at your new school. You will go from being a big fish in a little pool to a little fish in a big pool. Sounds scary right? Don't worry. You won't be alone. Everyone starting school across the entire country will be in the same position as you. And all those in the older years will have been in the same position just a few years ago.

TRUE STORY:

In my first week at secondary school we had a non-uniform day and one of the older girls came up to me. I was terrified but all she did was compliment me on my necklace and asked where I got it! After that she always smiled at me in the corridor and I was (hardly ever) scared of the bigger students again.

Lauren (15)

2: Second, your new school is likely to seem very large in comparison with what you have been used to. Long corridors, big halls and assemblies with hundreds of people- it might not be 'Hogwarts', but it is likely to be a little intimidating for your first few days. Don't be embarrassed to ask for directions, it's completely normal and most people will be very helpful and set you right.

3: Third, the range of subjects you will be studying are likely to be extensive and very new to you. As well as English and Maths you will also learn about:-

- ✓ Biology (studying living things like plants and animals, oh and us humans!)
- ✓ Physics (studying outer space and forces like gravity)
- ✓ Chemistry (studying chemicals and making experiments that go boom)
- ✓ Information Communication Technology/ ICT (learning to use computers, not just play games on them!)
- ✓ History (studying events that have happened in the past and why)
- ✓ Geography (studying the world and its people)
- ✓ Design Technology/DT (might be studying graphics, electronics or making things from wood or metal)
- ✓ A language (learning to speak and understand a language; probably French, German or Spanish)

OTHER CHANGES:

Form Groups: You are likely to be put into a form group or tutorial group on your first day. This is often done alphabetically. It is with this class that you will have registration every day. If you are coming from a very small school it may seem like a large group of students, but your class will always be around 30 people. You will probably have most of your lessons in your first year with your form group, so you will hopefully make some really good friends. Some schools have 'Houses' with classes from each year group. Again this is probably arranged alphabetically. These compete against each other in sports events and other activities.

TRUE STORY:

My favourite times at school are the House competitions. They're so much fun. The best is the 'Decorated Classroom Competition'. Each Christmas we have a whole afternoon off lessons to decorate our form classroom with any theme we want like 'Under the Sea' or 'Jungle Book' and then go and visit the other classrooms and see what they have done. The most original and creative wins lots of points for their House.

Suzy (14)

Class Sets

Each school is different. Some will separate you into different sets for different subjects in your first few years at school. This is done by looking at your test results and class work, or by your marks for your end of year exam. It can be useful to know that if you do very well in your subjects in your first year then you will be put in higher sets later in school and *might* get even better grades. Other schools will wait until you begin studying for your GCSEs in Year 10 (14-15 years old). Arranging students into sets is simply a way of making sure that you are with other students of the same ability level as you. This will help your learning and ensure you don't get too far behind in any of your subjects. Being put in sets also mean you will meet lots of other students who aren't in your class; another chance to make new friends!

More Changes

In addition you are likely to have more homework than you used to and there will be more tests and exams. Don't worry, you will adjust very easily and if you use the tips contained in this book then you will have no problems at all.

Some of the main differences will be

New Buildings   Bigger Schools   Older Pupils

Different Uniform   Different Subjects   New Teachers   New Friends

Getting to class

On your first day you will probably be given a <u>map</u> of the school buildings and maybe even shown where your classes are. MARK ON YOUR SCHOOL MAP WHERE YOUR CLASSES ARE!

Reading Timetables

One difference between primary school and secondary school is that your school day will be conducted according to a set timetable. Timetables are personal to each student and are likely to have the following information on them:

- ✓ *Your name*
- ✓ *All the subjects you have to study*
- ✓ *The room number and time where the lesson is taking place*
- ✓ *The name (or initials) of the teacher teaching the lesson*

They usually cycle every week or fortnight. They might look like this...

9.20 – 10.20	HISTORY		GEOGRAPHY	
	Room: 15	Teacher: T.T	Room: 8	Teacher A.D
10.20 – 10.40	Break		Break	
10.40 – 11.40	ENGLISH		BIOLOGY	
	Room: 2	Teacher: R.M	Room: 37	Teacher M.A.

So in this example, the lesson is:

- ✓ History
- ✓ in room number 15
- ✓ starting at 9.20 and ending at 10.20
- ✓ and it is taught by a teacher with the initials T. T

If you are having problems reading your timetable then try and work it out with a friend. If you still can't work it out then don't be afraid to ask other students or teachers. They will understand that you are a new student (don't forget they were new students once too) and will be able to help you.

TOP TIPS FOR THE FIRST DAY!

✔ Don't panic. There are lots of other students in the same position as you. You can all help each other out!

✔ Don't be embarrassed about asking teachers or other students any questions. This goes for questions about timetables or about your subjects. In fact, it goes for absolutely everything you think you need to know about.

✔ Use your first week to mark on your school map where your classes are.

✔ Note down where the school office is and if you are really stuck go there for help.

✔ Be friendly and SMILE! It will make you and others around you feel better and make a good first impression.

5. BACK AT HOME

With the tips in this book you will have survived your first day, and actually probably quite enjoyed it. Unfortunately, at secondary school you will have to complete homework most evenings throughout the week and over the weekend also.

Homework

OK, so nobody loves homework! It can take a long time, it's difficult and it's boring, right? Well, no actually.

Homework doesn't need to be difficult, boring or time consuming at all. In fact it won't be if you follow these important bits of advice. But first, it is useful to understand what the actual point of homework is. That way, when you are doing it, you will at least have some idea of why it has been set in the first place.

Why We Need Homework

Teachers are not as cruel as you think. They don't set homework because they like to make you suffer, or to stop you enjoying your life. In fact, you are given homework by your teachers because it is a valuable opportunity for you to practise what you have already learned in class. More than that, it gives you an important opportunity to learn to work on your own, without a teacher to ask for help.

> **TOP TIPS:**
>
> It is absolutely essential that you write down your homework clearly in your homework planner. If your school doesn't give you one, you can make one from a small A5 exercise book. Just write the days of the school week on the left side, draw a line down the middle of the page and write the exact details down on the left hand side.

- ✓ The subject for which the homework is set
- ✓ Any page numbers you have to read
- ✓ Any advice your teacher gives you on how much you should write or any advice on how to do the homework
- ✓ When it is due (it will normally be for the next lesson but not always)

For Example:

DATE:	SUBJECT	DESCRIPTION	DATE DUE
15th Sept	Biology	Write up experiment from today with diagrams, results and a conclusion	Tomorrow

If you **do not** write homework down clearly (and instead try and rely on getting the details off friends) then you are liable to make mistakes and get into trouble. It is much simpler to record it clearly and in detail when it is set.

IF THERE IS ANYTHING ABOUT THE HOMEWORK THAT YOU DON´T UNDERSTAND THEN ASK THE TEACHER STRAIGHT AWAY! This will stop you making mistakes and possible doing the wrong work.

TRUE STORY:

I once incorrectly wrote down the homework we were set for a History presentation. When my partner and I turned up to do the presentation we had both researched different topics. It was so embarrassing. Luckily, the teacher thought it was funny, but I'm always careful now that I know the right work to research from now on.

Paul (13)

Organising homework time

Homework doesn't need to take a long time or be difficult. Try following these tips.

TOP HOMEWORK TIPS

1. **_Listen in class_** – This will make your homework far easier to complete! Homework is always an extension of what you have been doing in class, so by listening well it means you don't have to re-read all the class material.

2. **_Do your homework the night it is set_** - The subject will be fresh in your mind (meaning you are less likely to struggle). Also, if you sit down to do your homework and are having problems with it, you will have time to ask your teacher or classmates any questions. Doing homework the night it is set will stop it piling up and prevent you doing the fun things you want to do.

3. ***If your homework is likely to take a long time (a long essay or geography project for example) then be sure to take regular breaks!*** - Every 1 hour take a 10/15 minute break in which you get a drink of water or eat something before starting work again. This is because you work most effectively in short spaces; you are less likely to make mistakes and the quality of your work will be better. Don't be tempted to have a break in front of the TV - that will only make your brain work even slower. You need a break to re-charge your batteries, start your blood flowing and get your brain back up to speed.

4. ***Choose the place you do your homework carefully*** - Don't do your homework in front of the television or with loud music on. If you really want to listen to some music try listening to classical music such as Beethoven or Mozart. This is because classical music has a repetitive pattern to it that helps you to concentrate on your work rather than distracting you every time the music or song changes. Just try reading a poem and listening to the radio at the same time, it's a lot harder.

Creating a good working space

Even if your room is covered in posters of your favourite footballer or singers it is important that you have a good working space where you can do your homework. A good working space will include

- ✓ A clear desk (without papers, chocolate wrappers and magazines strewn across it.)
- ✓ A good desk lamp (working in bad light damages your eyes.)
- ✓ A comfortable chair that supports your back.
- ✓ Peace and quiet so you can concentrate and get your work done quickly.

Put a sign on your door when you are doing your work- you don't want to be distracted by little brothers and sisters.

Think about it: the less distractions, the quicker you get it finished!

If it is impossible for you to create a good working space at home then think about doing your work in your school library (at lunchtimes or after school) or in the local library in your area. These will have great resources like books and Internet access for research, all of which are accessible if you register with them - it's easy, just bring your library card or some form of identification.

When and where should you do you your homework?

First, let's make it clear where you <u>should not</u> do your homework. Write down a reason for each of the situations below, saying why it is **NOT** a good idea to do your homework in these conditions.

- ✖ While eating your dinner
- ✖ While listening to your favourite band's new song at top volume
- ✖ In front of the TV
- ✖ Talking to your friend on the phone
- ✖ Lying on your bed
- ✖ Late at night, just before going to sleep

Instead, remember that your work will be better and more enjoyable (and take less time) when you do it when you...

- ✔ Are not in danger of getting interrupted
- ✔ Have a reward to look forward to, such as a game of football or watching a DVD with a friend
- ✔ Have set up a good working space (see above)
- ✔ Have drunk plenty of water
- ✔ Have all your pens and pencils, or a calculator nearby
- ✔ Have good lighting
- ✔ Take short breaks regularly

6. TAKING CARE OF YOURSELF

Diet

Your idea of a perfect diet might be chocolate and chips for breakfast, lunch and dinner. The reality though is that your diet should be balanced. A good diet is more important than you think!

Here's why…

- It makes it easier for you to concentrate - tasks like doing your homework or reading will seem easier to you
- It will prevent you getting ill. If you are fit and healthy you can do all the things you want to do rather than being stuck in bed
- It will ensure that you have enough energy to get through the school day, do your work and everything else you want to do

Here are the basics then. There are five food groups.

1. STARCHY FOODS: Breads, Cereal, Rice and Pasta

These contain carbohydrates, which are an essential source of energy, but they also contain important minerals and vitamins. Your diet should definitely contain this food group as it gives you energy. For longer-lasting energy brown bread, pasta or rice is better than white, but mixing and matching, that is eating some of what you like with some of what is good for you works well too.

2. FRUITS and VEGETABLES

Fruits are typically high in fibre, water and vitamin C. Your packed lunch should include an apple, orange or banana if possible, a great alternative to having a chocolate bar every day.

Vegetables are also really good for fibre, vitamins, minerals and all the things you need to keep you healthy and full of energy. If you find it hard to include them in your packed lunch, then make sure you have lots for dinner. A good solution is carrot, cucumber or celery sticks with a little pot of your favourite dip, maybe hummus, salsa or cheese and chive…

3. PROTEINS: meat, poultry, fish, beans, eggs and nuts

These foods are all sources of protein, which is essential for growth and repair of the body; this means they are great for energy and good for your skin if you're worried about getting spots! Be careful not to eat too many eggs or nuts as they are high in fat as well as protein.

4. DAIRY: Milk, Yogurt and Cheese

Milk and dairy foods such as cheese and yoghurt are also good sources of protein. They also contain calcium, which helps with strong teeth and bones, so soon you'll be as tall as all the bigger students you see around your new school. Again, some dairy foods like cheese are high in fat so try not to eat too much.

5. FATS and SUGARS

Fats and sugar can be sources of energy too, but these foods don't contain many vitamins or minerals, even though they often taste really good. But did you know that there are bad fats and good fats?

BAD (Saturated) fats are found in foods like pies, sausages, mayonnaise, butter, cakes and biscuits. Eating to excess, these can cause serious health problems and are also bad for your energy levels.

GOOD (Unsaturated) fats are found in oily fish like Tuna and Mackerel, nuts and seeds, avocados, olive oils and vegetable oils. These help your brain and body function better.

There are also two kinds of food containing **sugar**. Sugar is found naturally in things like fruit and milk. But sugar is added to processed foods like fizzy drinks, cakes, biscuits, chocolate, pastries, ice cream and jam. It's sometimes even in savoury foods like pasta sauces and baked beans. This doesn't mean that we can never have them, just that we should limit how much we eat or drink them.

Try getting into the habit of having a squash or fruit juice with your lunch rather than a can of fizzy soft drink. Juices contain far more vitamins and less added sugar than cans of drink (especially Coke). That means they won't make you overweight or rot your teeth!

Your school cafeteria should have a selection of foods within these groups but it is up to you to choose a meal that is balanced and nutritious. There is nothing wrong with having a plate of chips with your meal once in a while, but if you eat this every day then your diet is not likely to be balanced.

Your diet and your brain

Some foods are good for your brain, and some aren't. Oily fish, such as tuna and salmon, makes the cells in your brain thicker and so are excellent for your memory. Fruit such as bananas and kiwifruit helps brain waves to work more quickly, meaning you are sharper and more alert. Citrus fruit, such as oranges and lemons and green vegetables have lots of vitamin C which helps keep your immune system strong. That means your body can more easily fight off any infections that threaten it. Also, never forget that drinking plenty of water is one of the most important things you can do to stay healthy and feel great. Up to 75% of our body is made up of water and we need to ensure that we drink at least 2 litres of water a day.

Foods such as fizzy drinks and sweets are bad for your brain. They contain lots of 'E numbers', which are chemicals and colourings added to foods to make them taste nicer. However, these 'E numbers' are very bad for you and can make it hard for you to concentrate, or make you feel tired or grumpy.

TOP TIPS:

- Keep your **SALT** intake to a minimum. This means not adding too much salt to season food and also being aware that foods such as peanuts, crisps and pizza have lots of salt already within them.

- Never skip meals. It might be tempting to go hungry and save up your lunch money, but this will affect your concentration and eventually maybe your health as well. If you don't feel you have enough money without keeping your lunch money as well then you need to speak with your parents about the amount of pocket money you get.

- Consider taking a packed lunch to school. Lots of students do this. It can be a cheap way of ensuring you have a balanced and nutritious diet and stops you being tempted by chips every day! A typical packed lunch could contain sandwiches, an apple and a banana, a cereal or chocolate bar and don't forget a bottle of water or fruit juice to keep you hydrated! Try to limit yourself to one treat a day, you need the healthy food to get through the day, but it doesn't have to be boring! Try a fruit salad instead of just an apple, or a pasta salad instead of sandwiches, or crisps or vegetable sticks with your favourite dips. If you have time to help make your packed lunch it will help out your parents and make sure you get all the things you like in there too.

7. HOW DO YOU LEARN BEST?

How your brain works

Your brain has two distinct sides (or hemispheres) - the left side and the right side. Each side of the brain controls different types of thought. If you are a person who is more 'left brained' then you probably like to read, are good at maths and think very logically. You are quite rational and so can respond to situations with a well thought through argument and not with an emotional response only. If you are more 'right brained' then you are probably more intuitive and you act on your emotions and your gut-feelings more. You are likely to be more creative and thoughtful, capable of day dreaming wonderful thoughts and images, and putting those wonderful images down on paper as an elaborate doodle or painting.

Give some thought to what side of the brain you think is most dominant for you. There is no preference for one over the other- in our modern world we need logic and rational thought just as much as we need creativity and expression. Knowing how you naturally think can help you work on the areas you may need extra work on to improve.

Learning styles

We all learn in a different way and we have a *preferred style of learning.*

There are 3 learning styles:

Visual - This means that you like to learn best through seeing things- like *pictures, diagrams, images and colour.*

Auditory - These learners like to hear information and *verbalise it by talking it out loud.* They enjoy the sound of their own voice.

Kinaesthetic - Yes it is a big word! But basically 37% of us like to learn this way. That is by *touching, doing and moving.*

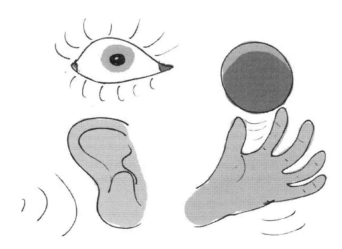

In many ways we use all 3 learning styles, but you will have a 'preferred' style – ever wondered what you're preferred style is? *Well just complete the following questionnaire and find out!*

Rate yourself on a scale of 1 to 5

*1 is **very little** and 5 is **a lot** – CIRCLE YOUR ANSWER!*

Visual Learner → *"I can see that it is right"*

Do you...?

1. Like to see information in a visual way I.e. mind maps, computers, graphs, charts, diagrams, videos and key words? *1 (2) 3 4 5*

2. Like to doodle scribble or draw? *1 2 3 4 (5)*

3. Highlight information by using colour pens or highlighting text on your computer? *1 2 3 (4) 5*

4. Prefer art to music? *1 2 3 (4) 5*

5. Like to set out information in bullet points or use 'post its' with key words? *1 2 (3) 4 5*

6. Prefer to be 'shown' what to do? *1 2 (3) 4 5*

Total .....21.........

Auditory Learner → *'That sounds good to me'*

Do you...?

1. Like to hear information by listening to tapes or use CD-ROMs/computer programmes to read out to you? *1 (2) 3 4 5*

2. Talk to yourself out loud? *1 2 3 4 (5)*

3. Learn best when you meet your friends and you can talk through the facts and figures you need to memorise? *1 2 3 (4) 5*

4. Enjoy telling jokes? *1 2 3 4 (5)*

5. Can recall what people have said accurately? *1 2 3 4 (5)*

6. Like to ask someone in the family to 'test' you on stuff you have learned? *1 2 3 4 (5)*

Total .....21.........

Kinaesthetic Learner **(yes, it's that big word again!)** → *'Let me handle that project'*

Do you...?

1. Like to work practically by touching and feeling *1 (2) 3 4 5*

2. Using computers to learn? *1 2 (3) 4 5*

3. Use your hands a lot when talking? *1 (2) 3 4 5*

Total....7.........

Check your scores and the highest result is most likely to be your preferred style of learning!

In the following section we suggest a number of different revision techniques. Check these out and see how they would be suited to your learning style. If you are an '**Auditory Learner**' then, as we suggest in the next section, use a dictaphone to record yourself speaking a language you study at school. Also, if you are an *'Auditory Learner'* then you will want to discuss your work out loud, wherever possible. You might try and have a group learning session with friends.

If you are a '*Kinaesthetic Learner'* then you probably work well with your hands. You are well co-ordinated and you like to dance, act or perform. Given that you learn well through movement you will want to try and incorporate movement into any learning you are doing. This won't always be easy (especially in the classroom) but try and throw a ball to yourself at home when reciting a poem you have to learn for English, or a set of French vocabulary for language class. Or try taking a walk, or playing with a yo-yo, at the same time you are reading some notes. You will also want to actually interact with the work you are doing. Little things like highlighting the most important sections of the work you are doing could help you learn better.

If you are a *'Visual Learner'* you will want to try and incorporate colour into their learning as much as possible. Make sure you always copy what your teacher puts up on the board and make your own mind-maps and spider diagrams (as discussed in the next section) of the subjects you are studying. Also, try and watch videos that bring text and words to life. For example if you are studying a Shakespearean text then you may want to try and find out if they have a film version of the text.

8. TEST AND EXAMINATION ADVICE

Tests and examinations are part of school life. Simple as that!

You might not like them, but you will still have to do them. If you take the advice set out for you in this book then you will be able to better approach tests and exams, in a more relaxed way. This will allow you to be more confident in your success.

In your first year at secondary school you may have tests to determine what 'set' you are in for some of your subjects.

There are some basic tips to taking exams that you should **ALWAYS** bear in mind:

1. **Listen to the advice of teachers.** Teachers will often give you direction as to what sort of questions will be in the paper and how you should answer those questions

2. **Prepare well.** If it is an essay subject test, such as an English exam, then try and prepare an essay beforehand, writing an essay under timed conditions. If it is a Maths exam, make sure that you know exactly how to use your calculator and are familiar with all the formula that might come up in the exam

3. **Know the facts about the test.** For example:
   - How long will the exams take?
   - How many questions do you have to answer?
   - How long, roughly, should I spend on each question?

4. **Never ever be tempted to cheat!** Quite simply, it is wrong. In addition, if that wasn't enough, you are likely to get caught and when you do you will get disqualified from the test as well as lose the trust and confidence of your teachers.

REVISION TIPS/APPROACH

Revising for exams or tests may be new to you. However, it's not that scary if you know how! You will soon find the most effective way for you to revise and it is different for everyone so do not worry if your friends do it differently from you. The most important thing is to find an approach that works for YOU.

Here are some suggestions for different techniques to try. You may find the perfect one for you or a combination of a few: just keep trying until you feel comfortable.

Before revision: Just like doing homework you need to make sure you have a good space to revise in, whether that is a room in your house or not. All your class exercise books, text books and a good supply of paper, pens and pencils will be useful. Remember what we talked about before, regular breaks (so your brain doesn't get too tired), lots of water and most importantly **PEACE AND QUIET!**

It is often helpful to pick just one topic to focus on at a time. Rather than saying 'Today I will revise all my Maths work'- it is better to pick one topic like equations and concentrate on that. Then you can have a break and maybe move on to another totally different topic (WWII history perhaps) afterwards. This can help as your brain will think in different ways on different subjects. If you stick to just one subject for the entire evening, you are likely to get bored more easily.

TOP TIPS:

If you have a subject you really don't enjoy try to make sure you have something to look forward to after you have finished working on it, like watching a favourite TV programme.

If you have a lot of different subjects to revise, some people find it useful to draw up a revision timetable so they can make sure they have enough time for each subject. If you do this remember not to panic if you need longer on some subjects, or if you finish one subject with time to spare that's fine. You will get used to the time the different subjects take and a revision timetable isn't like your class timetable, you won't get in trouble for changing it or not sticking to it.

Here is an example of a revision timetable. This will be different for everyone. Be sure to remember and leave space in your timetable for some fun and relaxing. If possible, use your longest break of the day to do something active- go for a run or take a long walk to get your blood flowing again and help your brain wake up.

TIME	SUBJECT
10.00-10.45	BIOLOGY – Plant cell structure
10.45-11.00	BREAK
11.00-11.45	ENGLISH – 'To Kill A Mockingbird' book revision
11.45 – 12.00	BREAK
12.00-12.45	FRENCH – Going to a restaurant/ vocabulary
12.45-2pm	LUNCH and football game

Different ways to revise

Here are a few _different revision techniques,_ Try them out and see which works best for you.

It's often a good idea to try out different ways of remembering things; think of it as exercise for your brain! It will mean you are prepared to revise in the way that is best suited for you when you get to your new school. You may find that different subjects need you to think in different ways.

1. Mind-maps / Spider Diagrams

These are great for subjects like History, Geography and Science. It makes you look at how different facts relate together. You can pick a topic, for example a play or book you are studying and try to think of all the things related to this subject and how they connect. The one below is a mind-map for thing that 'YOU LIKE':

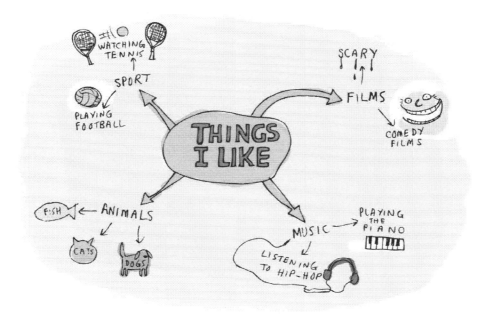

Now why not try to make one yourself in the space below. Just think of your favourite book, film, TV show, band, football club… it can be anything! Then try to think of related information and topics and see how they connect to the original. It might be a new way of remembering things for you!

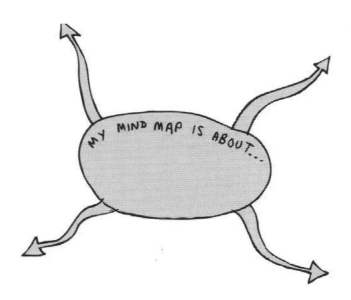

MY MIND MAP IS ABOUT...

2. Reading / Writing

Some people are lucky that they can remember things just by reading them or writing them out. This way of revising can be used for any subject. You simply write out your notes on the subject and then read them over. Then you can test yourself to see if you can remember or write it all down again without looking back at your notes. This doesn't work for everyone and can be a little boring! Try to include some drawings or funny stories to jog your memory.

TRUE STORY:

When I had to learn lots of the names for treaties (agreements between different countries) for my History exam, I ended up remembering them by funny phrases they sounded like. The Treaty of Saint Germaine in France became "Sam's yer man" because my brother's name was Sam. It really worked!

Claire (15)

3. Doing Questions

For Maths especially, the best way to learn how to do it is to actually do it. Just reading about it won't help if you can't do the sums yourself. Getting a revision book or even a different text book from school to practice questions will make sure you know how to work out each problem.

You could also get friends or family to test you on what you've learnt. Hearing questions phrased in a different way can really test if you have remembered it properly.

4. Dictaphone

Some people like the sound of their own voice! No really - it can help to record you talking about a subject and then listen back to it. You may notice any mistakes you have made and it can help you remember the facts better to hear yourself saying them. Most importantly, for languages like French and German you will have to speak out loud. So, why not get some practice in?

5. Revision Guides

You can buy lots of different revision guides that can be great for giving you different ways of looking at subjects and can include fun puzzles, quizzes and ways of learning new subjects. These can be bought at any good bookshop.

There are also great revision tips and help online for all different age groups such as:

www.cgpbooks.co.uk   **www.aqa.org.uk**   **www.bbc.co.uk/schools/bitesize**

6. With Friends

It may seem too good to be true but revising with your friends can really help, as long as you save the messing around until after you finish! Asking each other questions or talking about what you think of books or different subjects can help you to understand better and can be more interesting than just reading a textbook. It also means you have someone to enjoy your breaks with too.

7. Homework clubs

Some secondary schools or even local libraries will set up clubs where you can study with friends or classmates with a teacher or parent around to help if you get stuck. If you like the sound of this, but can't find one at school or in your area then speak to your parents or teachers about setting one up. They're bound to think it's a good idea and be very impressed with your enthusiasm.

9. SURVIVAL GUIDE

Using the tips we have talked about in the previous chapters you should have absolutely no problems settling into your new school. But of course, it is possible that things might still go wrong.

Behaviour and discipline

Each school has a different set of rules. Most of these rules will be basic common sense rules and will be very similar to the rules that you had to follow in your first school. However, some may be quite different, particularly in relation to uniform and how you have your hair or the amount of jewellery you can wear.

TOP TIPS:

Go on the internet and see if your school has a website. If it does then try looking through it and seeing if you can find a section with all the schools rules and uniform details. Print this section off and put it in your school folder.

There are certain standards of behaviour that you will be expected to follow whilst at your new school. If you fail to hand homework in on time, misbehave, or are late for class then you may receive a form of punishment. Each school will have different ways of disciplining students. Some of the most common methods are:

Detention

This might be at lunchtime or after school depending on what you have done. You may have to copy out lines (such as "I will not misbehave") or do homework in your lunch break or after school.

Tickets or Review

This is a piece of paper that you are issued which you take to each class. The teacher for the class signs their name and writes a comment about your behaviour in the class, noting whether you made listened well made contributions to the lesson and have completed your homework.

These are the milder forms of punishment! If these fail to mend your ways you may be suspended (prohibited from attending lessons) or expelled (also known as expulsion, where you have to leave the school forever). This is a very extreme course of action and one that no school takes lightly. Exclusions are few and far between. This does NOT look good on your school record however!

Your relationship with teachers

Try to remember that your teachers are human beings too. Just like you, they get nervous and tired, happy and excited depending on the situation they are in or how they are being treated. If you can always keep in your mind *why* your teacher is standing there in front of you then you are likely to have a far healthier relationship with them and, as a direct result, likely to find your time at school more successful and more fun.

So, what is your teacher trying to achieve standing there before your class? Well, the primary thing they are trying to do is to *give* you something. What is this gift? It is their knowledge and understanding of a particular area or subject. But your teacher is also trying to deal with the social situation before them, managing dozens of diverse and demanding students. This is a very stressful situation for anyone. Just as you have the freedom to make their life difficult, so they have the freedom to make your life difficult. If you can get on with your teachers you enable them to do their job. If you misbehave or disrespect them then you undermine their position and make life tougher for everyone, including yourself. Do everyone a favour and strive to understand what your teacher is trying to do. Then do your best to help them achieve it.

Try and remember the following:

- ✓ Treat teachers and other classmates with respect
- ✓ Follow instructions that teachers give you
- ✓ Respect school property and the property of other classmates. Do not steal or borrow items without permission

Of course it is your choice if you wish to misbehave! But the reality is that you will make your time at school much easier if you behave well and hand your work in on time. If you can establish a good relationship with your teachers, from the beginning, then they are likely to be supportive of you throughout your school years.

If you get a poor reputation then it can be hard to shake this off in later years. If you really can't do your homework for a particular reason then explain to your teacher as soon as possible. They are likely to understand if it is for a good reason.

Similarly, if there is a situation at home that might be affecting your behaviour or work, speak to your teacher about it. You should feel free to speak to them about *anything* - perhaps your parents are arguing a lot and it's upsetting you. Perhaps you are feeling unwell or anxious about something. Whatever it is, you should feel free to speak with teachers or other staff. Communicating with your teachers in this way might help keep you out of trouble.

Negotiation - how we survive in the real world

Negotiation is what many people call a 'soft skill'. And even though people don't really talk about it in schools (which is a big shame), being able to negotiate is one of the best skills you can ever have. You might say that being good at negotiating is about being good at getting what you want or need. But it isn't just that. Good negotiators recognise that the best way to get what you want or need is to help others get what they want or need too. What does this mean? Well, in negotiation we speak about outcomes being 'optimal'. This is the idea that an outcome can be better for the two people negotiating, not just one or the other.

Take this example. Say your bedtime is 9 pm. You think it is way too early, and want your parents to let you stay up later. Your parents have good reasons for not letting you stay up past a certain hour, or watching more than a certain amount of TV per day. However, it is also true that your parents want you to keep learning things and developing academically and more generally. Given this, you are faced with two possible choices:

A. You can confront your parents and tell them you want to stay up later. They will ask 'Why?' and you will simply say "Because I want to", or "Because my friends are doing it". Or alternatively…

B. You can approach your parents with a solution that makes everyone happy. What might that be? Well, think about what you want- to stay up late. And what they want- you to go to bed. But they *also* they want you to learn and develop knowledge about new stuff. So you can be creative and find a good *reason* for staying up later. You can go to your parents and tell them you are interested in learning more about a particular subject. It might be biology, or wildlife, or architecture (any subject that interests you!), and that you have done your research and found out that there is a BBC documentary on that subject every night from 9pm to 10pm. This, you would point out, will help you learn more about this fascinating subject.

Clearly, option B stands out as the better choice. You avoid all the problems that option A has: you don't get into trouble for 'confronting' your parents with no good reason to stay up later, and you avoid the real risk that your parents will just refuse to let you stay up. In short, option B is the optimal solution- *you* get to stay up that extra hour; *they* know you are learning about interesting new stuff. Everyone is smiling.

Negotiation is a great survival skill. We are always negotiating. We might negotiate over the game we play with friends on a lunch break- you want to play catch; they want to play netball or football. We negotiate with our parents - they want you to do your homework now, you want to do it in 40 minutes after a particular television program has finished. You will also negotiate with your teachers- you might be trying to persuade them to give you an extension on the deadline for a piece of work because you won't have enough time to complete it. You might have a family event - a sister's wedding for example- or something else that takes up too much homework time.

What does a good negotiation look like then? Well this is how a good negotiation will normally go:

- You think hard about what you want or need out of this situation.
- You think hard about what *the other person* - your friend, parent or teacher- wants or needs out of this situation.
- You work with that other person to try and generate as many possible ways to achieve what *you and they want.* You both try and be as creative as possible when thinking of these options- the sky is the limit!
- You think a little more carefully and consider which is the most *realistic and effective* of these options.
- You both decide to commit to your decision together.

The difficulty with negotiation comes from the fact that you will both feel that one of you has to win, and the other to lose. But that's very rarely true. That's why it's so important to communicate clearly with the other person. To work on your negotiation skills there are a number of things you should try and work on

1. Be a *good* listener - don't just hear what you want to hear. Listen carefully to what the other person is saying. Also, throughout the negotiation, remember to remain calm, receptive and respectful of the other person's feelings and opinion. Nothing is gained when we adopt a defensive or arrogant attitude!

2. Be an *active* listener - actually tell the other person that you understand what they mean; actually let them know what aspects of what they are saying you agree with.

4.   Communicate clearly - try and show the other person why certain options can help you both get what you want or need.

5.   Remember that while it is true that your goal is to try and convince the other person to say 'Yes' to what you are proposing, it is also true that you and the other person will get a lot more out of the whole situation if you are able to communicate and get a positive outcome for everyone involved

Bullying

Bullying is when a person or a group of people do things or say things in order to have power over another person. It can take many forms including name calling, ignoring a person, threatening them, making them feel scared, damaging their things, hurting them or forcing them to do something that they may not want to do.

There are lots of reasons why people bully. Often it is for getting attention, or to look good in front of others. Sometimes it will be because they have been bullied themselves in the past. Whatever the reasons, bullying is taken very, very seriously by schools and **must not be tolerated.**

Bullying can make people feel lonely, scared and unhappy. It can make them shy about making friends or contributing in class. When it gets really bad, it can make people not want to go to school at all. Don't allow yourself to be thought of as a bully! Nobody likes a bully, even if it seems like they might at first, they are usually just scared of being the bully's victim themselves. Be kind to people and accept that not everyone is the same as you. Whatever a person's race, religion or outlook on life they are entitled to be treated with respect.

Celebrate Difference!

Now it would not do if we were all the same - would it?

Just think how boring life would be if we were all clones of each other, all doing the same things and thinking the same thoughts. Some people are naturally quiet, loud or just like to be left alone. We all have our own ways of coping with life and there is no 'perfect way of being.'

It is important that when we meet people who are not quite like us that we don't give them a hard time for it! I am sorry to say that there are people who actually do just that. They make fun of, segregate or even physically hurt them. This is not acceptable and it will be considered 'BULLYING'. It is a very ugly thing to watch and an even worse thing to be involved in.

If you see someone being bullied then get them to speak to a teacher or, if you are being bullied, you yourself **must get help**. Do not suffer in silence. **YOU MUST DO SOMETHING ABOUT IT!** You have done nothing wrong and have the right to feel good about going to school and about yourself.

If you have already tried to ignore the bullies, or told them to stop and they have not, then there are a number of things you can, and *should*, do.

1.   Remember that *you* are not the problem...the bully is!
2.   Tell an adult. It could be your favourite teacher, the school nurse or your parents. If it is really difficult to talk about then write it down instead and give the piece of paper to an adult.

3. A lot of schools now have a new way of dealing with problems where you can go and talk to other older students about whatever is bothering you. This is a really good idea as you might feel more comfortable talking to someone closer to your own age. Also they may have been through the same thing as you or could send you to talk to someone who has.

4. Check out some information about bullying on the Internet. Try the following sites:

   ✓ **www.bullying.co.uk**
   ✓ **www.childline.org.uk**
   ✓ **www.dfes.gov.uk/bullying**

What if I feel like someone else is being bullied?

If you feel like someone else might be being bullied then you have to do something about it. Doing nothing sends a message to the bully and everyone else that bullying is ok. You should try talking to the bully or sticking up for the person being bullied, but perhaps the best help you can give is to encourage the person being bullied to talk to an adult.

Quiz:

What to do if you feel you are being bullied

Do you…   **A) Ignore them and hope they leave you alone**

B) Fight back and hope they learn their lesson

C) Talk to your parents or a teacher

What did you pick? It might seem obvious but often victims of bullying don't know what to do.

- If you picked **A** it is very likely that the bully would not leave you alone, if they think they can keep hurting you without you saying anything they may carry on.
- You may have thought **B** was the right answer and in some ways it is very brave to stand up to a bully, but it can also be dangerous and may not scare them into stopping.
- If you answered **C** you would be right! It's not running away or telling tales to talk to someone in charge about bullying, and any other victims will thank you for being brave enough to speak up.

Self-esteem

When we hear people talk about self-esteem, what do they mean? Well, the term self-esteem basically refers to the way that you think about yourself. A person with low self-esteem thinks that they aren't very valuable or useful as a person. They might focus on specific things they don't like about themselves, for example they might get upset about an aspect of their personality or a part of their body. It could be something like "My nose is too long" or "I'm too clumsy" or "I'm not funny, nobody laughs at my jokes"- the list goes on. Or their low self-esteem might be caused by the fact that they feel *different* from everyone else.

The truth is that nobody should feel like they are worthless. Nobody *is* worthless. It doesn't matter what you look like or whether you are in fact different; that should not lead you to feel like you don't have value. Having low self-esteem can be a real problem for young people. It can lead to depression (feelings of sadness that won't go away) or anxiety (continued feelings of uneasiness and worry).

What about people with high self-esteem? What do they think? Well, they also think "My nose is too long" or "I'm clumsy" or "I'm not funny, nobody laughs at my jokes". But then they do something else. They say "But that's OK because I like other parts of myself." "I like the fact that I am creative and quite good at Art" or "I like the fact that I have a good relationship with my sister, who I love very much" or "I like the fact that I can swim well"- anything really. They don't focus on the things they would ideally like to, but cannot, change.

Remember that nobody likes everything about themselves- nobody! So if you find yourself thinking that you are worthless, remember that **you most certainly are not.** Our advice would be- try to avoid being a perfectionist. Not everything you do has to be absolutely perfect. And anyone who thinks that it does (it could be a parent or a teacher) is simply wrong. *You* don't have to be perfect! We will say it one more time because it might be the most valuable thing you ever hear- *you* don't have to be perfect! So, always try your best with homework but don't feel too bad if you try hard and don't get great grades, particularly near the beginning of secondary school. School is about learning and you aren't expected to know everything already. Don't be the person who is terrified of failure and never takes any risks. It's good to take risks as long as you learn from them. And try and work on your ability to accept criticism. It's OK for people to not like everything about you, the way you probably don't like everything about them. That's life. Did we mention that you don't have to be perfect?!

So think of your self-esteem like a muscle in your arm or leg. If you keep working on it, it will get bigger and stronger. We aren't pretending it is easy to learn to accept who you are and, strange as it sounds, to love yourself. In fact we *think* it might be the hardest thing you ever have to do. But we also *know* that it will be the most important.

10. YOUR LIFE OUTSIDE THE CLASSROOM

Yes, there is life outside the classroom! Believe it or not secondary school is not just about learning academically - far from it. There is a whole range of exciting and interesting things you can do when you are not in class. Extracurricular activities will be great ways of meeting new people, making new friends, challenging yourself and, ultimately, growing into a healthy, happy person. One of the ways you can be active outside of the classroom is to join one of the various clubs or societies that your school will offer.

Joining Clubs and Societies

Each school has heaps of different clubs such as sports teams (football, rugby, hockey, netball, tennis), chess clubs, debating societies, Maths clubs, film clubs...the list goes on! Just think about what you're good at, what you enjoy doing, or even something you might never have tried, but would like to.

Clubs and societies are free to join meaning there really is little reason not to look around and find a club or society to join. They may meet at lunchtimes or after school and can be a great way to meet people and make friends. By joining different clubs you are likely to meet people from other year groups and classes too, having something else to do apart from academic work can be a great way of letting off steam and relaxing.

Remember what we said earlier about concentration and taking breaks? It is always a good idea and can actually help the quality of your work when you eventually do sit down to do it. Another bonus of joining clubs and societies is that it can look good on your school record. You may, after a few years or so, be given some positions of responsibility within these clubs and societies. Maybe you will be made captain of the netball team or chairman of the debating society. This will look good when you are applying for universities later in your school career. But the most important reason for joining is simply to have fun!!

The Internet and Social Networks (Facebook etc).

Gone are the days when you had to wait until the following day to talk to your school friends. Now, through the beauty of social networking sites like '**Facebook**'/ '**MySpace**'/ '**Twitter**' you can easily keep in touch after the final school bell rings. Many social networks have age restrictions, but you may know people who have set up their own accounts or you may have even set up one yourself. If you do use social networking sites you should know a few very important rules.

First of all, many schools have banned access to these sorts of social networking sites. Don't try and access them in school time.

Second, be very, very careful what sort of material you post on these sites. Do not share personal information such as bank details (if you have a debit card for example) or post photos or any other information to people you do not know (ensure your privacy settings are set to strict on the sites you are using). Also, remember that comments and posts on sites such as '**Facebook**' are very hard to interpret in the way that you meant them to be interpreted. What seems like a joke to you may not be treated as a joke by someone else, and that someone else may just include your teachers. Any comments which could be interpreted as racist, sexist or in any way amount to bullying others, will get you into serious trouble and could even cause you to get thrown out of your school. Keep your online conversations polite and never post anything that could upset someone.

Third, a golden rule you should never forget. Never make any comments at all about teachers. Your friends or people within your class may set up a '**Facebook**' page or group about a teacher. Whether the point of the page is to be kind to the teacher ('Mrs Smith is the best teacher ever' or cruel to the teacher ('Mrs Smith is the worst teacher ever') you are *strongly* advised not to join or interact within this '**Facebook**' page or group.

Fourth, the Internet is a great place for you to go and find out information on topics for your homework, or to read more generally on an area you find interesting. It is a great resource that your parents never had access to when they were young (yes, they *were* young once). But you must be very aware that there are dangers online. Some older people pretend to be younger people online in order to get you to share information with them - always be very careful that who you are talking to is who they say they are. Stay on the sites that you know are safe and, if you are online without any supervision, only ever access the sites you would be comfortable visiting if your parents were with you.

Also, never think you can get away with simply copying information from the Internet as a shortcut to completing your homework. This is something teachers are always looking out for and they will almost certainly realise if you try and do this - it's simply not worth the risk. Use the Internet to help you do your work by all means, but never try and use it to cheat or trick a teacher as you will get in trouble for this.

FINAL WORDS OF WISDOM

Here are some final words of wisdom that we can give you about your move and about growing older more generally. If you have read this book from cover to cover you are more than ready to get underway with secondary school. You should be excited- you are going to enjoy yourself!

However, just to recap it is useful to sum everything up at the end of the book...

TOP 5 TIPS

✔ **Remember that you have 2 ears and 1 mouth.**

That means you listen twice as much as you talk. The more you listen the more you will learn and understand.

✔ **Always give 100% to work you have to do both in the class and for homework.**

Go over it again either by asking the teacher or talking to friends about it.

✔ **Be a good listener to others and try and appreciate what they are saying to you and think about how you can help.**

✔ **Don't listen to verbal put downs from others – they are probably just jealous and want to undermine your confidence.**

Remember

YOU'RE A STAR

and...

...KEEP SMILING!!!

ABOUT THE AUTHORS

Maria Adams has over 30 years experience teaching in secondary schools and a master's degree in Education with a specialism concerning children with learning difficulties. She also has a graduate diploma in Counseling.

Martin Adams is a graduate of Harvard University as well as universities in both England and Australia. In addition to teaching in the UK, he has taught younger children in an orphanage in Cochabamba, Bolivia, and he is a Board Member at C.A.S.A- a non-profit network dedicated to representing the best interests of children who have been removed from their homes due to abuse or neglect.

Together, they have taught children from ages 7 to 15, and run numerous innovative courses on study skills, child psychology and preparing children for their move to secondary school.

Printed in Great Britain
by Amazon